WHILE IN THE
Waiting Room

While in the Waiting Room

By Cherrylean Johnson Givens

While in the Waiting Room

Good News for Your Heart and Soul

Cherrylean Johnson Givens

Publishing Group

A division of Thomas Nelson Publishing

Since 1798

www.wpublishinggroup.com

Dedication

This book is dedicated to:

My husband, Bishop Jerry Givens

To the love of my life, you have been by my side through thick and thin, through all my waiting periods, even when I did not think I could handle some of the assignments that were chosen for me by God. You are my strong human tower. My family means everything to me. My husband is my world. Mother told me to get someone who loves you more than you love them; whatever you do in life, make sure it is something you can live with. When we first met, he was such a lady's man I did not want everybody's man. I wanted my own man, so he was ready to step into the light and serve one woman and he chose me. He was most definitely, worth the wait.

 Thank you for making me your Queen, for you will always be my king.

Cherrylean Givens

While in the Waiting Room

Chapters

While in the Waiting Room

Introduction

August 11, 2020 - English Language
Learners **Definition** of **wait:** to stay in a place until an
expected event happens, until someone arrives, until it is
your turn to do something, to hope that something will
happen soon.

 Waiting, have you ever felt like you have been placed on a
waiting list all your life, stuck in a waiting room, holding a
ticket with your number on it, but before they get to your
number either they, run out of time, or the last one was
just sole, or its closing time so you have to come back
tomorrow and try again. I am not saying this is the story of
my life, but sometimes it feels like it.

Let's start from the beginning. I am the 13th child out of 18
children, so I have had my share of waiting for things;
when you're raised in a big family such as mine, it seems
you have to wait for everything. We waited on our turn to
get to the bathroom, to ride the bike, to go to the grocery
store with mother. I had to wait on the hand-me-downs
that your sisters could no longer wear or wanted to wear.
Then there were times when you had to wait on your older
sisters to get ready when you have been ready for at least
thirty minutes, or you had to wait on your younger siblings'
either by cleaning up behind them, or cleaning them up,
again. So, you were stuck in the middle between the older
ones and the younger ones. I found myself once again
sitting in the waiting room.

Please don't misconstrue, I loved my life growing up in a big family because it taught me so much about how to love and be loved, how to share and share alike, it taught me humility and patience; I learned my best social skills in this big family God blessed me with. I learned how to forgive and be forgiven, how to lose and how to win. I learned about peace. War and survival skills. It taught me how to be a daughter, a sister, a mother, a wife, and most of all, a friend, and a family.

So, my friends, this book is not about my family; it is about life, particularly my life. I want to share how life itself can bring out the best in one or the worse in one, some of the things we may or may not encounter while we are in the waiting room of life. Waiting is a process, it is like going through the stages of life. Because life is all about having patience and waiting, we must wait to be born 9 months to be delivered, give or take. The cycle of wait goes on No matter who we are, we all experience the waiting game.

CHILDHOOD

Waiting As a child, I found myself in the waiting room a lot. There were 12 siblings ahead of me in our house; we had to wait in line for everything. At least it seemed that way, we had to share a lot of things from toys to clothes. Are any of you familiar with the term hammy downs? You had to wait for clothes to be passed down from your older sister or brother. Maybe you had to wait your turn to sit in the front seat. Yes, waiting has its pros and cons.

I learned a lot from my childhood experiences; my daddy would always say to me, "Never put all your eggs in one basket; you just may trip and fall and crack them all." It took me a while to comprehend what daddy was saying, then one day; I figured it out. I stop putting all my hopes and dreams in one thing or one person, you will find yourself in their waiting room or on their waiting list.

Waiting for a speedy recovery. I can remember one of the longest waiting periods of my young life, was when I had an accident on my bike. I was about the age of 10, I was riding my bicycle "really fast" on a country gravel road on my way to the neighborhood party store. Along comes two semi-trucks racing. I tried to turn toward the ditch. I thought to myself I rather fall in the ditch, I'll come out with maybe a busted knee and a few scratches. When I began to turn the wheel toward the ditch to avoid the trucks, my handlebar striped and I went toward the trucks into the traffic, one truck hit me, the other truck drug me some feet; they tried their best to avoid hitting me, everything happened so fast. I think I lost consciousness; when I woke up, I was in the hospital. I had three holes in my head; the doctor said after a head injury, as vase as mine, brain function can be temporarily impaired, which can lead to difficulties such as seizures, dizziness, fatigue, depression, irritability and memory loss. He also told my parents that if I live through this, my chances were slim and I could be a vegetable for the rest of my life. However, when I woke up, I knew my name, I knew my mom and dad, God was so merciful to me. My parents had to wait with anticipation with prayer and supplication.

Waiting to be released from the hospital, the worst was over for the doctors but not for me. I had to go through recovery; you may have heard the saying," It gets worse before it gets better." So True They had to shave all my hair off. I remember waking up crying in the middle of the night, the bandages sticking to my pillow from the blood draining from my incisions in my head, I had repeated headaches, I couldn't stand bright light and a lot of loud noise. I had to stay home from school for a long time, the waiting was driving me crazy. I believe it was the first time I was vulnerable to depression, I didn't understand it but I had it big time. Some days, I just cry, cry, cry. Some night I tried to stay awake all night long afraid I would not remember anything or anyone when I woke, and so afraid I would not wake up at all. Sometimes to take my mind off things, I would try to remember how my life was before the accident.

I was a very active little girl, no different from any little girl my age. I was always climbing a tree, playing ball, or just running around the neighborhood. All that fun was part of my life that had ceased, and I had to sit in the house looking out the window watching the other children play. I really thought I would never be a normal little girl again. So, I had to be rushed to the waiting room.

One positive thing I do remember about this waiting period is that I had a lot of moral and family support. They slowly nurse me back to health. The doctors continue to monitor me for symptoms of delayed brain trauma; with regular CT scans of the brain, I had to continue doing various mental exercises, such as crossword and word games. My family kept me active by engaging me in physical exercise when I was ready, they read to me and they also made me read to them out loud and we did lots of puzzles. I guess that's why my children love doing puzzles to this day. Thank God for blessing me with a loving family. The song says, "Love lifted me when nothing else would help love lifted me,"

Waiting to recover, I was able to return to school. I did fall behind in my grade, and it took a while for my hair to grow back; that was another waiting period for me. The loss of my hair made me feel a little ashamed and incomplete, I had to wear scarfs or hats. I never will forget the day I was able to put my hair into a ponytail once again; looking in the mirror, it was like a new birth for me; my emotion was all over the place. I didn't know whether to smile or cry; I was too young to understand those feelings, now that I'm older I think they call them "mixed emotions." All I could feel was just being happy to be normal again and that I was able to get back in the swing of things. I learned so much throughout this waiting period, they are patience, compassion, humility; most of all, I learn the power of pain and that time does help heal wounds. The good times of adventures outweigh the unpredictable times.

Waiting on mom and dad to come home. I know it may sound crazy but I was one child who never wanted to see my parents leave the house because I always had a fear of them leaving and never returning. I was paranoid. I didn't know the meaning of that word back then, but that was me. I would cry whenever they left without me; I remember sitting on the porch some days waiting for mom and dad to come home from whatever journey they were on to the doctor's office, to pay bills, the grocery store, etc. I would sit at the window waiting for dad to come home from work. I would pray as a little girl, God please send my daddy home safe. There were so many of us in the house, I was afraid that they would get tired of taking care of us and just take off and leave us with our older siblings to take care of us. So, whenever they left the house, I would go into a panic if they didn't return at a certain time. I found out later that one of the reasons I was afraid of mother and dad leaving the house was because the day I got run over by those trucks, mommy and daddy were not at home, and I was afraid that something like that would happen again.

Waiting for a change in every season of our lives, we must wait on something or someone, take the microwave for instance, yet it's faster than the conventional oven, yet we must still wait on it. We wait on cold food to get hot and hot food to cool. That is life. Waiting is a part of life; it helps to develop us. It teaches us patience, which is something we all can use a little bit more of. Waiting does not always seem good, but it is always good for us; others may look at waiting as some form of punishment, like the child that is asked to go to the time-out chair that sits next to the teacher's desk. Waiting is a form of discipline, not punishment. From a child's view, Yes, some may feel like waiting is all I do. Waiting is a period of learning. I remember two main events during my childhood days as the longest waiting period. It was waiting for my birthday and waiting for Christmas. Yes, waiting is a hard thing to do especially when you are a child. Waiting has this strange dynamic. The more you wait, the longer time will stretch. Mother used to say, "A watched pot never boils," and a watch clock never moves."

Waiting to overcome the guilt, children experience so much throughout life, some things are revealed and some things never revealed. I have always been fascinated with the piano. I dreamed of being a great piano player one day, and with a family as large as ours we just couldn't afford a piano, so some days after school, I would go to this church to practice on the piano, I felt safe there, some days I felt like I was in piano heaven, some days the pastor would step inside just to hear me play, he would always clap when I was done and encourage me to keep up the good work. As a child, you are always looking for a place of protection, a place to love and be loved. What better place than the church, if you can't feel safe around the church or the man of the cloth, who can you feel safe around? After all, in a child's eyes, he was the closest thing to God. One day my life made a complete change that day he came and sat next to me while I was playing. When I finished, he applauded as usual but after the applause, he ran his hands up my dress. Yes, sexual assault and sexual abuse isn't always sex, yet it is illegal for an adult to touch any portion of a child's body with lascivious intent, improper touching is still a crime. You suffer emotional stress even though you were just touched inappropriately

Statistic says that "one in four girls and one in seven boys will experience some form of sexual abuse before the age of 18." I was that one; it has also been said that children are usually abused by someone they know, I found that to be true. I can't even imagine what could have happened if I hadn't run away that day, and although I broke away from the perpetrator, the emotional scars and effect seem to last a lifetime. That day running and crying all the way home, left me feeling dirty; I felt like I was to blame. It's amazing how one moment can change a person's life. My biggest regret was that I never told my parents what happened, I just tried to dismiss it out of my mind, so I carried this burden throughout my life. It diminished my trust in men, that day I went home not even feeling safe around my brothers, and even my own father. I didn't feel safe around any of my male friends or my brother's friends, it caused me to build a wall of protection around my body and heart. I had so many questions in my mind. Will I ever be able to trust again? Will I be able to trust a man of God again? I even wonder within myself if there is a God, and if there is, why did he let this happen to me? Why didn't he protect me? Now that I am older with a family of my own, I have learned more about sexual abuse, so I could teach my children and hope that they would never have to experience this. One advice I have to give is if this happens, cry aloud and spare not, tell everyone you can. If one person doesn't listen, tell someone else until you get results.

Everyday I waited for that healing of the mind and the heart, I was too young to know what forgiveness was all about, so I don't even know if I could forgive. I was so afraid, so confused, one thing I did know how to do and that was to pray. Some days I found myself just staring into space; as I relived that moment over and over in my mind, many days I tried to replace the thoughts with a good thought or a happy song. I was afraid that if I told my dad, he would do something bad to him and have to go to jail because my dad owned a gun. I didn't want to lose my daddy, so I kept it inside all those years, until one day we had a (YWCC) meeting at our church, Young Women christian Council and the topic was how to overcome hurt, one young begin to share about how she was molested by her father, God spoke to me and said this is your day to overcome by sharing your story with the council, at first, I said I can't do that I'm the first lady, they are going to look at me differently. I did answer to the voice of the Lord, and when I finished, there was not a dry eye in the room; that was the day I got total healing. Yes, the waiting game has always been a part of my life, and I know it may be a part of your life also because waiting teaches us patience. "And patience, experience; and experience, hope: And hope maketh not ashamed because the love of God is shed abroad in our hearts." Roman 5: 4-5 (KJV). Jennifer Lewis said, "When your heart is hit, don't quit."

TEENAGER

I remember those days well. I always found myself trying to be as good as my sisters and friends. I tried basketball, volleyball, and cheerleading. I wanted to be a cheerleader because my big sister was one. So, the next year I tried out. I knew I was a shoe-in because only 10 of us were trying out; cool they only needed 10 they must pick me to make the squad complete. To my surprise, the next day for tryouts, 11 of us showed up; they called everyone's name but mine. So, I went out for track; I was naming Cherrylean Johnson the most valuable player. I really don't know if I got that title because of my performance or because I was the only black runner on the team that year. Do not misconstrue me; the teammates were nice, the coach was nice but down in my heart, track was not for me.

Waiting to be liked by others. I liked singing in the choir; music was my passion, still trying to find myself, what makes me happy and what will make my family so proud of me. While in the waiting room, there were so many people I looked up to and desired to be like; one of them was my cousin Joyce. For many years, I watched her in the marching band at the football games she was a majorette boy was I fascinated by her and how she twirled that baton, one day, I expressed to her how I wish I could do that, she replied, "you can but it takes a lot of practice, and then she said I'll teach you, I was so ecstatic I didn't know what to do; she said I have a spare one you can have.

I practiced with her all summer the next school year; I tried out for the majorette squad and guest what, they called my name. That was the first accomplishment in my life. That year, I decided to wait and not try out for cheerleader instead, I settled for the least competition, and I ended up not liking it that much at all. It wasn't what my heart really wanted.

Waiting on maturity I am sure that many of you have at one time in your life experienced little girls crushes where you like someone, and he does not even know you exist. Or the puppy love phase where you like him, and he likes you and five other girls in your classroom, so you are placed on the waiting list, hoping he chooses you to be the one.

Throughout my teenage years, I waited to be accepted by my peers; I got into the church at the young age of 15. Most of my classmates were not into church. Yes, some of them went to church. Church was a safe haven to me. I love going to church because I felt safe, so I gave my life to Christ; I am reminded of the one scripture they drilled into all of us "Children obey your parents in the Lord, for this is right. Honor your father and mother (which is the first commandment with a promise), that it may be well with you, and that you may live long on the earth" Ephesians 6:1-4 (Bible).

Waiting to cultivate my passion, the church is where I began working with children. I loved being around the older mothers and I love working with the children; that is where I discovered my passion and call to be a teacher of young children. Yet, I still struggled with insecurity. I was waiting on something great to happen to me. Yes, getting saved was one of the greatest things that could happen to me, but I was waiting on God to do things that I needed to do for myself, so I found myself back in that waiting room.

God spoke to me and said, just like you study to get good grades in school, you must study the word and learn of me. So, I begin to read my word every day. I would ask God to guide me in the word, I begin to learn what the scripture means by, I can do all things through Christ who strengthens me." My faith began to get stronger and my confidence got better. While in the waiting room, I waited on a lot of things as a young woman.

My last two years of high school were the best; I was able to graduate with honors despite what the doctor said, despite the peer pressure, and believe me, there was a lot of peer pressure. I realized that it took a made-up mind. I can hear my dad saying, "if you don't stand for something, you will fall for anything." That year I walked across that stage not only a virtuous young woman but a virgin young woman and a victorious young woman. While in the waiting room, do not fret for God is not through with you yet. The sky's the limit; never give up hope and always have faith that there is someone out there for you, so do not settle. The bible says that "patience is a virtue."

While in the waiting room, some of us can't wait to grow up before our time; instead of enjoying the age we are, we try to act older, or we want to rush through some of the stages of life that are in the plan of human nature, my perspective as a young teenager was that I had to learn to love myself more than anything else and more than anyone else. Once I concord that battle of not wanting to grow up too fast, not trying to keep up with others or not trying to fit in with others, and trying to be someone else. I learn to just be me, and I found out that in my perfect imperfection, I am at my best when I am being me, "Simply Cherry."

CAREER

Waiting on a career. Have you ever had a big dream of what you planned to do when you finished high school? Well, like most teenagers, I had a plan for my life. When I graduated, I was going to do like the Beverly Hillbillies. I was going to "Load up the truck and move to Beverly." Well, it did not quite happen that way; I don't think my dad was too happy about me not going; he wanted me to just at least visit my aunt and uncle in California, just the experience alone would be good for me, seeing I have never been anywhere other than Louisiana to visit my grandmother. Most people go off to college, then get married and have a family; that is the American dream for some women. Well, I kind of rearranged the order of life, I got married first, then my husband and I went to college together, my dream was to be a teacher or a professional singer. However, because my counselor noticed that my high school transcript and my report card reflected that I had outstanding skills in the secretarial ream, she suggested that I take up intro to business and secretarial field, so at her advice, I did just that so I'm in the waiting room once more. I put my dreams on hold, I did get my Associate degree in business and clerical Secretarial.

Waiting On Job My first job was not what I wanted, but it was what I was qualified for. It complimented my degree. I got a job working at the hospital in medical records; day after day, I went into work unhappy, feeling incomplete for two years. I stayed in that waiting room until one day I was invited to assist in a Montessori Classroom. I literally fell in love with what I had been exposed to as a new way of teaching children, so that year, my boss asked me how I felt about becoming a headteacher, I was ecstatic, so I enrolled in Adrian Mi. because there is free tuition, not even a college loan available like for other colleges I had to pay out of pocket upfront my tuition in full, I received my Associate Degree as a certified Montessori teacher. I taught there for two years.

Waiting For Success, I have always wanted to own a daycare and one day my own Montessori school, so I went to Rochester, Mi and received my Bachelor degree in Montessori to teach Elementary 1-4th grade I. Later I opened my own daycare and Montessori kindergarten school in my home 1995, I decided to become my own business owner that is what my college council suggested. I could not afford a building of my own, so I decided to open one in my home. I renovated my family room for the babies and my garage to accommodate the pre-school children, what a milestone in my life. I could never imagine the feeling I felt when I got my letter in the mail from the child care license that I was approved. The journey begins for "The Giving Tree Daycare," years of a dream come true, loving and doing what I have a passion for caring for and teaching children. Oh, how well do I remember watching the children crying and clinging to their parents, afraid to let go, afraid to trust me or their new environment? Yet, I also remember the day they dropped them off to the daycare and they jumped into my arms no longer afraid that my home felt like their home.

 Waiting to celebrate my career was complete, I thought. We were embarking upon our 5th year anniversary of being in business; we had a wonderful staff; everything was going great until we got hit unexpectedly with great devastating news. It was one Saturday morning I got a phone call from the grandparent of a family of children we supplied daycare for. This family was more than a customer, they were like family. I shall never forget those words spoken to that morning on the phone. He said to me, "If you're standing, you need to sit down, he proceeded to say" my babies are gone, all of them including their mother." At first, I thought he meant gone, moved out of town and he began to tell me what happened. I dropped the phone and began to just scream and cry, I couldn't stop crying. My husband had to come in. I couldn't even tell him what happened. He picked up the phone and began to talk to the grandfather to get some clarity. He told us that the mother and all four children died in a house fire that morning. I never saw that coming, we had plans for the children to come over that morning. And I was blindsided by the Phone call I received. Having to attend that funeral was one of the hardest things I ever encountered in my life. I had cared for those children ever since they were six weeks old, so you can imagine their ages rein from 6 to 1. I kept them 8 hours a day, 5-6 days a week. I was technically their second mother.

Waiting to be healed. Their death made such an impact on me that I had to close my daycare down for a while because the emotional mental trauma was just that great. Some days, I would sit and cry to myself, "they never said I'm leaving you, they never said goodbye." Trying to forget the tragedy that changed my life forever. It was such a dark place in my life, someone had turned out all the lights and

I could not find the switch. Death leaves a heartache no one can heal; love leaves a memory no one can steal" God had to speak to my mind and my heart and I heard Him say one day, there are many children like them that still needs your care and love, are you going to give up on all children because I choose to love them more than you, I replied, "yes Lord, I hear you."

Waiting, I went back to school, got my master's degree in education and opened a Montessori School called the St. Ruth Montessori Academy. This school catered for all children who were struggling or held back in the public school. My goal was to help children of all grades excel back to their rightful grades so that they could graduate on time. The school also had a preschool and kindergarten program for the young ones. Because when I had my daycare, I catered for Infants and I also had a Montessori program for preschool to kindergarten. So, I wanted to continue that in memory of the Hoyle Grandchildren.

WIFE

Waiting to be chosen, nobody wants to be overlooked or rejected; the problem with waiting to be chosen is that there is a possibility you may not always get what you bargain for. So many women are still in the waiting room, looking out the window wishing that someone would soon come along. In your mine your saying my biological clock is ticking away, wondering when is my number coming up?

Waiting for Mr. Right Ladies, you know how we all have dreamed of meeting our Prince Charming, the one who will one day come and sweep you off your feet. Yes, ladies' dreams do come true if you are willing to wait. I remember it well when this young man walked into my life and respectfully introduced himself to me. It took me by surprise because I was not looking nor was I pursuing this. It was like something was happening that I was not prepared for. I was back in the waiting room for two years of engagement. That means everything and all things considered, we know it is becoming almost a thing of the past. I believe the word called "Celibate" abstaining from marriage and sexual relations, typically for religious reasons." (Dictionary) To me, it was more of a principal thing. My mom taught me not to save sex until marriage "that your body, your future, and your life are things sex cannot control for you if you wait until marriage." So that worked for me. While in the waiting room. When you give respect, you earn respect.

Waiting Becoming someone's wife is a life-changing experience; you go from daddy's little girl to another man's wife; that's a lot of adjustment, in one life at one time, your routine changes, from caring for me, myself and I to caring for us. Caring for another individual is easy when you are in love. You do not mind sharing your meals, your time. Loving this other person unconditionally, physically, and emotionally, no longer could I just focus on how I feel, I had to take the other person's feelings into consideration. Yes, the role of a wife is crucial because in those early stages of marriage anything you do or don't do, anything you say or don't say, can either make or break the home atmosphere, so as the woman you are constantly striving to adjust to that big change because you want your marriage to be a success. I could hear some of my friend's voices saying girl, you have to lose to gain; they were not ready to be anybody's wife because you must give up too much of yourself. Not true becoming a wife does not mean losing myself or my identity. I still did some of the things I enjoy doing, I still have a social life, my special time alone and we both have the same beliefs and values.

Waiting to be approved, my husband and I were very young when we married, we were both brought up in Christian homes, and although he was saved when we married, he knew more of the world than I did. I was a little country girl, with no experience. So, everything we did was through trial and error. Some say my mother taught me how to be a wife. I just watch her and I emulate what she did for my daddy. This is true to a certain extent, I say you can watch a person drive a car everyday all day, but until you actually get in the driver's seat and drive for yourself, you don't know how it feels. It has been said, "that practice makes perfect." I had to practice being a wife; I learned in my early stages of marriage that what works in one women's house may not work in my house and some of those things did not work in my marriage. So I have learned throughout these 45 years of marriage that it has been said "to never let the sun go down on the raft," and as the bible states, "Wisdom is the principal thing and all thy getting, get understanding," KJV. It took a whole lot of work and patience for me to get where I am today. I have learned to support my husband in all his ventures and endeavors. Even when some of them seem like the twilight zone, even when I did not understand what was happening, or what was going to happen or if anything was going to happen at all. Sometimes, I would say to myself, this wife thing is a tough assignment lord and I know you understand what they meant when they said, "that love covers a multitude of fault." Marvin Gaye said, "sometimes it makes me want to holler and throw up both my hands" and Johnny Cash said, "you got to know when to hold them, know when to fold them and know when to walk away." So many days, I found myself saying, "Lord, I need your help right now."

There have been times when it seems like everything I did or tried to do was wrong, no matter how hard I try. If I disagree with him, it appeared that I was being disrespectful to him, and yes, a lot of times it, was my fault and a lot of times I was wrong. Wrong in my thinking and wrong in my actions. I can remember hearing my mother say, "you can get anything out of a man if you present it to him right." Yes ladies, it's all in your presentation. The bible says, "a soft answer turns away wrath." KJV. I had to remember that it was not what I said, it is how I said it. I know Patience does not come easily in a marriage because things are no going to go like you want them to all the time, so when things do not go as plan, I remind myself

25

that we are in this together, and "together we stand and divided we fall." So I'm still standing as a Wife.

MOTHER

Waiting There is no role in life that is more important than that of a mother. Everything I am today is because of my mother. Becoming a mother transforms the life of a woman, from a pampered carefree, sometimes selfish girl into a heart-changing, responsible and unselfish, ready to take on the duties of motherhood. The degree of life's severity differs from person to person. It takes so much to wait; even though I had a delivery date for my daughter to be born, she came two days later than the due date, then to add to that, I was in labor for 24 hours, oh the agony of waiting was so severe but She was definitely worth the wait. They say that a mother's work is never done; from the time your baby enters this big place called the world, the cycle begins. Baby must wait for mommy to feed her, burp her, change her, bathe and, pick her up and cuddle her. Then as time progresses, the tables turn, and the mother cannot wait until the baby starts talking, crawling, and walking. It is all about the waiting process of life.

A new journey begins when you have children, you tend to have to go more, cook more, spend more, and clean more; you do what you can to make it work. Children quickly become the most important thing to us. family is everything; raising children takes a lot of your time and attention and sometimes takes priority over your own personal desires. A young growing family can and will add additional complexity. In our family there were 18 children, one day I ask my mom why did she have so many of us she said, "well daughter, if I had stopped at 12, you wouldn't be here today," case you all didn't know I was number 13 so on that note, I told my mom I am so glad that you decided to have my other 5 siblings after me. I thank God for the 4 children He blessed me with Anna Marie, Latonya, Jerry Jr. Erica, Ruth. My children have made our lives complete. They are the joy of our life—children are important. They are our future! As the role of mother, we have been given a responsibility to Love, Teach, and Protect them. We should invest time in our children by being involved with them, investing time in them, letting them know how much we love them and how much God loves them.

Waiting to be more, being a mother means more than just cooking and cleaning, doing laundry, you know the normal chores, duties, and routines that a mother is known for doing under the heading of mother. To be a good mother, we must first focus on ourselves before we can take care of others because a family can only be happy and healthy if the mother is happy and healthy. Do not overwhelm yourself by trying to do too much in too little time. Sometimes mothers burden themselves with too many responsibilities. My dad would often tell us, "never bite off more than you can chew." I had to learn that the hard way, mothers learn to delegate and use the blessing God gave us, which made us mothers in the first place, children it's ok to take a break and relax and let the other family members of the house help lighten the load of motherhood. If you take my advice, it will keep you smiling, and a smiling wife will be the most pleasing thing to see for a husband returning home from work who had a hard day.

Waiting to become the perfect Mothers. First, let me start by saying there is no perfect mother because we strive to be that which is impossible, we are often misunderstood, and when it comes to raising children, mothers don't necessarily always know what's best, and conflicts between children and mothers is a part of life, yes mothers will always feel like their children are going the wrong way or doing the wrong thing, so they have to make it right. We think being a good mother means sitting in little chairs with our daughters playing make-believe tea time, or even throwing the ball to our sons in the back yard or trying to teach our children all about life. All this is important and is a part of being a mother. "The good, the bad and the ugly." While so many mothers have lost their children or never had them at all, I thank God for Motherhood.

Waiting to differentiate, mothers often must play the dual role of wife and mother; trying to separate the two and put them in their prospective places gets confusing sometimes. I remember as a young mother some would address me as Jerry's wife or Anna, Tone's, Jerry or Erica's mother, so for a long time, I didn't know I could be anyone else. Don't misconstrue; being a wife and mother was one of the most rewarding things I ever achieved in my life. It also was some of the most challenging moments of my life, just knowing that I was solely responsible for Loving and caring for another human's life scared me to pieces. I could never imagine loving someone as much as myself and sometimes even more than myself. I would never trade this feeling for anything else in this world. Nothing can take the place of the greatest adventure life can give, motherhood. Through all the surprises, all the chaotic moments, all the identity crises, the sweat and tears, motherhood brought out the best and the worst in me. I think that motherhood is one of the greatest gifts from God. I can hear mommy saying, "don't sweat the small stuff daughter, embrace the simple things of life." Being a mother enhances who you are; it brings out your best and your worse, your strength and weakness.

I FOUND OUT ONE DAY THAT I COULD BE JERRY'S WIFE, ANNA, TONE, JERRY JR., AND ERICA'S MOTHER AND SIMPLY CHERRY ALL AT THE SAME TIME.

FIRST LADY

It was in 1986; I was just a 29-year-old girl when I got the news that my husband was going to have the mantle passed to him instead of his older brother James. Yes, his father was retiring from the office of Pastor of the Prayer Garden COGIC. He said that God had already shown him in a dream that he was going to be asked to take on the task of Pastorship, so when his dad came to us, he was already mentally prepared by God. On the other hand, I had no clue. I was blindsided and after hearing that news, I was one emotional rack, full of tears, anxiety. I was one scared young lady; I thought within my mind, this is all a dream and I'm going to wake up soon. I had experience in College, Career, Wife, Motherhood, yet with all these credential's I feel like none of these had prepared me for this newly appointed elevation called the first lady. While talking to myself and talking to God, the question that came to mind was, where do I go from here? Somebody tell me please. I knew about wearing many hats, as a church worker, I song in the choir, I was on the usher board, the nurses' gill, the (YWCC), Young women's Christian Council, being a part of each of these auxiliaries changed my life in such a positive way, yet none of the previous are comparable to how my life was about to change as first lady.

Waiting on the answer to this new phase of life. I know that every level of life brings about a change, but this was not puberty. I was too old, nor was this midlife crisis because I was too young. There were so many questions running through my mind. Somebody help me. Is there a class that teaches you how to be a first lady? Sign me up. Am I dreaming? Please wake me up? Lord, I was not looking for this nor was I waiting on this. What is expected of me lord? Am I fit for this position? Why me Lord? Why not me Lord? Lord, I need your help. So I found myself in the waiting room again as a First Lady, trying not to get in anyone else's space while trying to figure out what was my place. Trying not to offend once again trying to fit in, I felt like I was among strangers, but I was with people that I have known for 12 years. We prayed together, shouted together, broke bread together, and traveled together. We were a Christian family; the scripture says, "How can we sing when we're in a strange land." KJV. I felt like I was in a strange land. It was like the twilight zone. There were days when I wanted to walk away but the Lord said, "Cherry Stay,'' so I listened to the voice of God and I asked Him for help and guidance. I remember making one request of him; I said, God please don't let me hold anything in my heart.

Waiting to do me. I admired both of my mothers, my birth mother, Velma Ruth Johnson, was a kind woman. She taught me so many things about life, how to be a loving and caring person; I watched her down through the years, take care of her household, her family and her husband. I looked forward to coming home from school every day finding my mother in the kitchen cooking and singing. She was a perfect example of the Proverbs 21 women in the bible, and as much as I loved and adored my mother, I never tried to walk in her shoes. I always wanted to make my own footprints and follow my dreams. What I loved most about her is that she supported me in everything I tried to do. She never tried to make me walk in her shadow and I love her for that. She always wanted me to be me.

Then there was my mother-in-law Ruth Givens, she was also a beautiful woman inside and out, she dressed with grace and fineness when she spoke to people and listened to both men and women, she was a lover of people. She was a loving mother, seamstress, a supporter of her husband and a beautiful first lady. She had great influence over the women in the church. When she opened her mouth, she would sing with such power and anointing. To me she was also the perfect example of the Proverb 31 women. I never wanted to walk in her shoes either, although some of the people may have felt differently, I only wanted to be me, Simple oh Cherry.

Waiting for equality, as a first lady somedays, I felt worthless. I battled constantly to build myself up, trying to keep myself mentally stable. I struggled with low self-esteem and insecurity. As a first lady sometimes, I felt like the last lady, always having to take the back seat or turning the other cheek, and no matter what I did it, did not measure up. I found myself talking and singing to myself, encouraging myself just to get through the day. I had to constantly remind myself that I only have one life to live and I am going to live it to the fullest not according to the way someone else expects me to live. I began to struggle with this new position of first lady. I was being judgmental even before I really got to know what it was all about. I realized I was just as bad as the people I served by not giving God a fair shake and trusting in Him who had bestowed such a task on me. The life of a first lady is not all a bed of roses, yet it is not all doom and gloom either. I will say that it is a humbling experience to some and an exalting experience to others. Although equality sometimes is never achieved at all times by the people, it is good to know that God sees us all equal in His eyesight. The late Dr. Purvis Givens, my father- In- law often told us, "if you do good, good will follow you," the bible says, "do unto others as you would have them do unto you" (KJV). So, in my daily walk as first lady Cherry, I humbly ask God for His guidance and help. My motto is: "Only what you do for Christ will Last." I forever keep that humble question in my heart, that famous quote from the Winan Brothers "Lord am I doing your will, or should I just be still?"

I remember the Late (Mother Leana Mason Lucas) walked up to me one day and put her arms around me, and gave me the biggest hug. She said, "Daughter, just show love in everything you say and do; everytime your enemy comes up against you, let them see love, love the people of God unconditionally and you will be alright. Just lead by example and they will follow your lead." I can hear my mother's voice saying, "do what you know to do; what is truly in your heart proves who you are. Love and even when things look unpleasant around you, the love you have inside will give you strength to get through all that is going on outside of you." "Whom God calls he qualifies" KJV.

SINGER

Waiting to sing, as a little girl, I always loved singing and hoped one day I would be a great singer, every day I would sing in the tub back then; we did not have showers to sing in, so I sing while taking a bath. One thing that kept me in the waiting room of becoming a singer is that I was afraid we often had talent shows at school. My brother Ameal would get on that stage and sing and dance just like the Famous James Brown and he would win the crowd. My first time singing in front of a crowd was in the church. My dad would make me get up and sin; I will never forget the song by the Caravans Lord Don't Move My Mountain. I would cry and sing at the same time. I was the opening act for my brothers group called the Johnson Singers; they traveled from state to state singing the gospel. What seemed to be a bad situation for me turned out to be good. The bible says, "All things work together for good" (King James).

Waiting to be inspired. I remember the first time I got to lead a song in the church choir; It was at Coleman Temple COGIC; that was a scary moment for me because I was so insecure and afraid. I remember worrying the night before and trying to figure out how I could get out of singing this song today. I guess you're wondering why I felt this way, you have to know the history. Those Coleman temple singers were one of the most popular and group of singers in the city of Saginaw, they were born singers, their mom and dad both had profound singing backgrounds. The late Dr. Hurly Colmen Sr. and Dr. Edna Coleman. The children inherited that talent from their parents, so I was afraid big time, but the choir director encouraged me so much, she told me, "I was going to be okay; she said just do you, be yourself," and I did just that. Thank you to the late Hurly Colmen for those wonderful words of encouragement, they meant the world to me. The Coleman family has always been a great inspiration to me and my brothers the Johnson. I love singing the church choir; at nap time, I would sing to the children. They did not want me to just play the naptime cd I had to sing along with it for them to go to sleep. When I was younger, I used to hear my oldest sister sing her name was Rose Marie. She was a writer and a singer, when she sang, she sounded like an angel. I admired her, so I used to ask God to help me to sing like her. She was my greatest inspiration; there has never been a time I am inspired to write a song that I do not think of her. We lost her in 1977; that was the first time I experienced losing a loved one. It was tough for the whole family. She will forever be missed. I love you Rose Marie, your sister Cherrylean.

Waiting to share the gift that God had given me, it started in the late seventies at my own church Prayer Garden cogic, that was where God opened the door for me to inspire other young people to pursue their musical desires and talent, as I mentioned before I love singing but singing was not my only passion, I loved playing the piano also, so I started out singing in the choir and giving private piano lesson to children in the neighborhood at my home. Every day I would get on my piano, sing and play. It gave me great joy to help others. Some of them could not afford to pay for a lesson, so I just started giving the lesson free to anyone that wanted to learn. Just hearing them play and seeing the smiles on their faces brought great joy to my soul. I remember my father in the gospel saying, "we have to be great enough to let someone else be great." I am so Godly proud of one of my students' name Bernard Jackson Jr. who was very dedicated to his conviction. He is now an independent producer and music engineer. He now has his very own studio and music Company entitled "Brainstorm Entertainment."

It has been said, "that the difference between good and great is exposure." As an educator, I would tell my students that there is no one-size-fits all in education; as a teacher it is my job to meet the needs of every student in this class, so it was necessary for me to find out what type of learning style each child has. Likewise, there is no one formula for the music industry, but I would like to share with the next generation of Gospel Music makers, five encouraging steps that helped me along the way:

1. Get involved locally, that is, giving back to the community. Join a community choir; I have been a faithful member of the Flint City Wide Choir for many years.

2. Develop a plan and be persistent.

3. Make a demo of your best effort, put your best foot forward in everything you do.

4. if any of your material is original, have it copywritten first and don't expect to get it back.

5. Remember that when meeting people in person, you are your own best packaging.

Waiting on my next assignment, this phase of my singing career started at the Prayer Garden cogic, with a group called the "Prayernetts" the original group consisted of two families the Givens and the Jacksons, Ramona, Carla , Darla Jackie, Sherry, and later Monique and Tonya joined the group. I started out managing this group of talented young ladies and I mean talented. Each one of the girls had a unique sound, but once they blended those voices together, it was an amazing sound to the ears. I remember the many rehearsal days, many concerts, and then it happened. I can't tell you how, I can't tell you when, but somehow, I ended up singing with the group. I believe I started as a fill-in because one of the girls couldn't make the performance and the rest is history. I love singing in the background until one day, one of the girls suggested that I lead a song that they heard on the radio, that was my first lead song with the group called the prayernetts. Success was written all over this group but somehow, time and space got in between this group and they never were able to reach that goal. Life changes bring about a change. We sang together for over 10 year. I know between losing a member to replacing a member, all and all, it was one of the most rewarding times of my life and I never regretted a moment of it; since then, some have relocated, but those that have remained in Michigan every now and then we do a throwback and we come together and perform for old time sake. To my girls, the prayernetts you are the best.

Thank you for allowing me to practice on you guys as a leader, a manager, and a singer; you will always be my unsung heroes.

Waiting to sing again. Some of my favorite singers and great performers are Mahala Jackson, Shirley Ceaser, Vicky Winnan, Lisa Paige Brook, Dorinda Clark Cole, and Karen Clark Sheard, Dottie Peoples, just to name a few. It has always been my dream to one day be a part of this gospel view. Ever heard of the phrase "you are your biggest hinder?" well, that was me; I was my biggest critic and my biggest battle was fear, so here I am again, traveling with this same old giant, fear. Fear of rejections, fear of not being accepted, fear of not being good enough to compete with the cast of gospel singers of today. That fear kept me in the waiting room until one day, something miraculous happened in my life. I shall never forget, I mentioned earlier in this chapter a young man named Bernard Jackson Jr. That I used to give free piano lessons when he was a teenager. One day, I got a phone call from this young man, he told me that the Lord had given him an assignment to do, and that project involved me. God told him to Produce a CD with Cherry Givens. At the time, he lived in Atlanta and I lived in Michigan, but somehow by design, I just happened to be going to Atlanta for a Women Convention that same week. Talking about the fruits of your labor, who would have thought?

Waiting to record again, I had recorded once before with Bernard Jackson and Tone Givens when the company was called T-Boon Production that was about 10 years prior, but this time it was different, I arrived in Atlanta and in seven days, we had a finished product, entitled "Simply Cherry" I came back to Flint for the finishing touch on the project, my daughters, my son-In-law with the company of a few others critiqued and edited the project, with the expertise of Bernard Terry the chief engineer mixed and mastered it. This was only the beginning; this cd gave me a platform I had never experienced before. Someone once said, "the difference between good and great is exposure." With the powerful single at that time, "Stand." This song was written by me under the guidance and the influence of God; this song was birthed during one of the most trying times of my life. So many changes, a new life, new family, new surroundings so much was happening in my life, many nights I laid awake wondering how I was going to make it through and the Lord spoke to me in a soft still voice "stand still and know that I am the Lord." So whenever I found myself facing something new, I begin to sing the lyric to the song, "Stand when you have to stand alone, stand when all hope seems gone, stand through the storm through the rain, stand for you know your labor is not in vain, standing on the promise of his word." This song has brought me through many trials, my best friend moving away, the loss of my oldest sister Marie, then my Loving brother, Wendell, then my loving parents, it wasn't until the loss of my mom that I decided to dedicate this cd to mom and dad.

Waiting to be included. The only thing I regret is that my parents never got a chance to hear my cd or see me on the Bobby Jones show. I can hear my dad's voice saying, "Cherry, you are just as talented as those other singers, don't sit on your gift." Since then, I have been blessed to release four more cd's "So Amazing," "Holy," "Cherry Merry Christmas" and my latest "Mirror Mirror" I must say it has been challenging both mentally and financially to try to stay afloat when you are an independent artist. But through it all, I have learned to trust in God. He has given me a great team of workers; Bernard Jackson, has stuck by my side through thick and thin, now my biggest fear is that I will never measure up or get that big break because of the lack of financial supplies, yet he never waives his faith in me and the God I serve. I know that God has a purpose for my life, He knows my passion for singing, it's not about making the almighty dollar; I love what I do, ministering to God's people is what I was born to do. I just want to make my mark in this music industry for my family, the Johnsons/Givens, my children, and grandchildren. I want to leave a legacy. My advice to young upcoming artists would be to never give up on your dream because dreams do come true. God except your praise, no matter how small it may seem to others. Hope is alive and well and "hope maketh not ashamed" (Roman 5:5) KJV. God, I would just like to pause for this moment to take time to thank You for loving me unconditionally and allowing me to be a vessel and a servant for You and Your people; it has been an honor and a privilege. Thank you for choosing me to be in this waiting room with You, as my guide and protector, while in the process, You have shown me my purpose, You have helped me to develop the many gifts You have blessed me with, and You said in Your word that "my gift will make room for me" (Proverbs 18:16) KJV.

BISHOP'S WIFE

Waiting for the transition after the initial shock, I finally came to the realization that I am who I am and it's going to take some time for me to do what Michell Obama says "get comfortable with a little greatness." Once again, I am at the crossroad of doubting my own worth in God's eyes. I find myself repeatedly saying believe in yourself and trust God, don't try to do what you know you can't but do what you can do best, and find your own voice and place in this new stage of your life. Never happened, some may look at becoming a bishop wife as the highest achievement in this Christian life; I agree. The bible says, "to whom much is given, much is required." I finally see why it was necessary for me to be born in a large family of 18 children, my purpose of becoming a minister's wife and then a pastor's wife, although there was no instruction or script on the duties of any of those positions one thing I know with a shadow of doubt is that I was born to serve.

Waiting is a process of life who would have thought that I would be in this position, not me, we were tossed in the waiting room for this elevation by the prophecy of the late Bishop Walter E. Bogan. We had attended a special service at Harris Memorial; the guest for that night was Mr. Clean. That night after service, we were asked to accompany Bishop Bogan and his guest for a repass. It was at that repass that Bishop leaned over and said to my husband, I see you up here with me. You are going to be a Bishop. That was in 2000, I did not see it then, the human part of me felt doubtful, but I would never share how I felt to my husband. I wanted to encourage and support him in all that he accomplished in this journey of Christian life.

Suddenly God spoke to me in that moment of doubt, encouraging me to stop focusing on what I cannot see if God has promised you something even if you can't see how it is going to come to pass. "God is not a man that he should lie neither the son of man that he should repent hath he said it and shall he not do it or hath he spoken it and shall he not make it good" KJV Numbers 23:19.

My husband, as modest as he is, just took it as a compliment coming from the Bishop, and he felt honored just to be in fellowship with the Bishop and his guest. At this time, we were in the North Central Jurisdiction under the leadership from 1984 t0 2010, when the bishop retired, the mantle was passed to Bishop Drew Sheard, we remained faithful from 2010 to 2016. We went on with our everyday lives as Pastor and first lady, serving the people of Prayer Garden and the Flint community. Saturday, January 30th, 2016, my husband was led to recruit Superintendent Don W. Shelby Jr. to start a fellowship; when superintendent Shelby was approved to become a Jurisdictional Bishop, Bishop P.A. Brooks recommended my husband to Bishop Shelby as a candidate to become an Auxiliary Bishop.

So here we are, nineteen years later, the prophecy has been fulfilled how our only wish was this, that Bishop Bogan could have been here to share the moment of his prophecy unveiled, but somehow, I feel that he was looking down on my husband saying that's my boy, So here I am trying to walk in these shoes, as a Bishop Wife, on this journey I have been exposed to so many great Bishop wives in my lifetime, that has impacted my life. I want to recognize two of our most loved Bishop wives of

Michigan/Ontario that I personally became acquainted with, that are no longer with us, the late Mother Iola Williams and Mother Willie Mae Sheard. I must say that it's an honorable blessing and a wonderful feeling to be a part of such a great cloud of witnesses, the Bishop Wives. I know that throughout the waiting periods of my life, it was all for God's glory.

WAITING ON THE WORLD TO CHANGE

Waiting on the change of the world, in the biblical days we were under the slavery of King pharaoh waiting to be freed, God sent Moses to the rescue, the struggle for freedom is an ongoing battle. That touches every race. In the workplace we fight for economic freedom that would mean more jobs. We fight for better schools for our children. In the forties and fifties, we were under slavery by the white masters, again fighting for our freedom, the civil rights movement, waiting to be freed through the help of Abraham Lincoln and Harriet Tubman, war on drugs and for criminal justice reform. Then in the late fifties, we fell into the slavery arms of that mighty king heroin; I Must say that in my lifetime, I have literally seen it all from the civil rights movement. Respect for the dignity of each person is the foundation of moral and social progress.

I was born in the fifties, I came up at the time Racial discrimination was at its full bloom. Racism is an age-old problem that still exists not just in the black community but in the church community as well. I was raised in the church, or as some may say, I was raised a Christian. I have seen so much in my lifetime from this world. I know what it was like to raise my children in this never-changing world, how it was a challenge to raise a family in time like these to teach my children to be intelligent for my daughter to be a woman and my son to be a man, and waiting on my children to walk into their calling. No matter how much we tried to shelter them, we could not keep them from experiencing some things in this unchanging world. The church used to be a safety net but there were people in the church that you couldn't trust that we had to protect our children from also. So, I weep for my children and my grandchildren. The waiting room kept me on my knees praying and hoping that one day I could help make this world a better place for them to live in.

Waiting on equal rights law, that every citizen of the United States would have equal rights, to not just vote for the president, but we have held the office of the president. to use the same restrooms, drink out the same fountain, same hotels, eat at the same restaurants. Not only do we eat at the same restaurants, we are now owners of some of those restaurants. Thanks to Rosa Parks, no more sitting in the back of the bus, to first come, first serve seating. We are no longer just actors for the white man; we are directors and studio owners, African American historians, scholars, educators, and publishers. I believe that Black lives matter. I believe that all lives matter. yes, it happens in the workplace, in the schools, in the colleges, even in the political arena when we are not judged by the intelligence of our character but by the color of our skin. This place called America the land of equal opportunity. It is a constant battle. Someone once said, "that everywhere you go, there is trouble," so where do we go from here? I guess we just have to wait patiently for a change to come. Some want to skip the waiting and just fast-forwarded to the process.

Waiting for normality to return to this world after the pandemic. The 1918 influenza pandemic was the most severe in history, which was caused by an H1N1 virus.

Which brought the world to a complete stop? Now we are faced with the Covid 19. This pandemic has put us all in the waiting room at the same time. We all were blindsided at the same time. Never did we ever expected to be in this type of waiting room, but here we are with "151K, Covid cases and 7,227, Covid Deaths in the United States alone, once again a pandemic has brought the world to a complete stop. We are trash into the waiting rooms of our homes, living in fear of the unknown, now going on nine months that we have been incarcerated, prisoners in our own homes, separated from the world and even separated from our loved ones. Some say God is trying to get the attention of the world because our world is moving at such a rapidly fast pace. We want everything done fast, quick and in a hurry. We had no patience for no one and no respect for anyone. Some feel that He is trying to get the attention of the church because they have left their first love, and "the love of many has waxed cold." There is such a vast display of self-righteous and political movement being practiced within the church; Messages are centered around prosperity and blessing have been manipulated to preach a man-centered gospel. And not a God-centered gospel. So, because of lack of responsibility, God has placed us, the Christians in this waiting room to teach us how to seek Him again.

So as the old saying goes "Patience is a virtue." Waiting helps to birth out patience, so here we are not at our own will, but at the will of the unknown that we are forced to wait whether we like it or not, and yes, it's a humbling experience for all of us, we are no longer free to do as we will because now the governor rules once again. So, we now must wait for permission to go forward in life with restrictions. We try to go along with our daily tasks, trying to make ourselves feel like things are back to normal when they are not while worrying about what the future holds or wondering within our minds will some of us even live to see the future. So now we're on our knees crying out, waiting for God to make the next move, to come to our rescue, this world is broken and the situation seems hopeless, so we keep waiting for the world to change, waiting for the problem to be solved, waiting for the pain to go away. Some people progress while in the waiting room while others digress, while in the waiting room, I am waiting on my next assignment from God.

WHILE IN THE WAITING ROOM

While in the Waiting room is a continual series that journeys throughout my lifetime. Starting with a young girl growing up in the apple tree county of Carrollton, Michigan, even then, I was being groomed for my recent role as a supporter and partner in the fellowship of God's call on my husband's walk in the ministry. As a woman living in a modern world, we are often faced with putting our lives on hold while assisting others with theirs. My first role as a preacher's daughter, then-wife, and now mother and grandmother showed me all too many times the undying selfishness that women have to face being the lesser vessel. This book was created to display the living testimony of my life to help other women as they are waiting on change and waiting on God while In the Waiting Room

WHILE IN THE WAITING ROOM

CHERRYLEAN JOHNON GIVENS